ANIMALS

Maddie Spalding
and John Willis

www.av2books.com

AV² provides enriched content that supplements and complements this book. Weigl's AV² books strive to create inspired learning and engage young minds in a total learning experience.

Your AV² Media Enhanced books come alive with...

Audio
Listen to sections of the book read aloud.

Key Words
Study vocabulary, and complete a matching word activity.

Video
Watch informative video clips.

Quizzes
Test your knowledge.

Embedded Weblinks
Gain additional information for research.

Slide Show
View images and captions, and prepare a presentation.

Try This!
Complete activities and hands-on experiments.

... and much, much more!

Go to www.av2books.com, and enter this book's unique code.

BOOK CODE

AVP29778

AV² by Weigl brings you media enhanced books that support active learning.

Published by AV² by Weigl
350 5th Avenue, 59th Floor   New York, NY 10118
Website: www.av2books.com

Library of Congress Cataloging-in-Publication Data
Names: Spalding, Maddie, 1990- author. I Willis, John, 1989- author.
Title: Animals. All about summer / Maddie Spalding and John Willis.
Other titles: All about summer
Description: New York : AV2 by Weigl, [2019] I Audience: K to grade 3 I Includes index.
Identifiers: LCCN 2018053475 (print) I LCCN 2018059511 (ebook) I ISBN 9781489696793 (Multi User ebook) I ISBN 9781489696809 (Single User ebook) I ISBN 9781489696779 (hardcover : alk. paper) I ISBN 9781489696786 (softcover : alk. paper)
Subjects: LCSH: Animal behavior--Juvenile literature. I Summer--Juvenile literature
Classification: LCC QL751.5 (ebook) I LCC QL751.5 .S668 2019 (print) I DDC 591.5--dc23
LC record available at https://lccn.loc.gov/2018053475

Printed in the United States of America in Brainerd, Minnesota
1 2 3 4 5 6 7 8 9 0   22 21 20 19 18

122018
102918

Project Coordinator: John Willis   Designer: Ana María Vidal

Every reasonable effort has been made to trace ownership and to obtain permission to reprint copyright material. The publishers would be pleased to have any errors or omissions brought to their attention so that they may be corrected in subsequent printings. Weigl acknowledges Alamy, iStock, and Shutterstock as the primary image suppliers for this title.

First published by The Child's World in 2017

ANIMALS

In this book, you will learn about

what they are

what they do

how they change

and much more!

Keeping Cool

It is summer! A rabbit rests in a burrow. Shade keeps the rabbit cool.

🌎 Many rabbits in Wyoming and Montana live in Bighorn Canyon. They look for food at night to stay cool in summer.

6

A turtle warms itself on a rock. Then, it slides into a pond.

Summer is hot. Animals do not need as much fur. They shed their fur to keep cool.

A wolf has **two layers** of fur. It sheds the inner layer for **summer**.

Animals find food in summer. Flowers bloom. Hummingbirds drink nectar from flowers.

Plants grow.
Deer eat the plants.
They find plenty of food.

13

Grizzly bears eat fish.
They find seeds and berries.

A grizzly bear may eat **90 pounds** of food in a **single day**. (41 kilograms)

Bees collect nectar from flowers.
They bring it back to their hives.
They turn it into honey.

Some animals change color.
Arctic foxes turn brown in summer.
This helps them sneak
up on prey.

19

Some hares also turn brown. This helps them hide from predators.

Alaska hares are
some of the
largest hares
on **Earth**.

Pom-Pom Hummingbird

Make your own pom-pom hummingbird!

Supplies:

- 1 toothpick

- 1 muffin cup

- 2 large pom-pom balls

- 2 googly eyes

- glue

- black marker

- scissors

Instructions:

1. Use the marker to color the toothpick. Cut the toothpick in half.

2. Glue the pom-pom balls together. Glue eyes onto one ball.

3. Cut the muffin cup into four equal pieces. Glue one piece on each side of the pom-pom ball. These are the wings.

4. Glue one piece of the muffin cup onto the bottom of the pom-pom ball. This is the tail. Glue the toothpick half on as a beak. Now you have a hummingbird!

KEY WORDS

Research has shown that as much as 65 percent of all written material published in English is made up of 300 words. These 300 words cannot be taught using pictures or learned by sounding them out. They must be recognized by sight. This book contains 47 common sight words to help young readers improve their reading fluency and comprehension. This book also teaches young readers several important content words, such as proper nouns. These words are paired with pictures to aid in learning and improve understanding.

Page	Sight Words First Appearance	Page	Content Words First Appearance
4	a, in, is, it, keeps, the	4	burrow, rabbit, shade, summer
5	and, at, food, for, live, look, many, night, they, to	5	Bighorn Canyon, Montana, Wyoming
7	into, on, then	7	pond, rock, turtle
8	animals, as, do, much, need, not, their	8	fur
9	has, of, two	9	layers, wolf
11	find, from	11	flowers, hummingbirds, nectar
12	eat, grow, plants	12	deer
15	day, may	14	berries, fish, grizzly bears, seeds
17	back, turn	17	bees, hives, honey
18	change, helps, some, them, this, up	18	Arctic foxes, prey
20	also	20	hares, predators
21	are, Earth	21	Alaska hares

Check out www.av2books.com for activities, videos, audio clips, and more!

1 Go to www.av2books.com.

2 Enter book code. A V P 2 9 7 7 8

3 Fuel your imagination online!

www.av2books.com